THE LITTLE PINK BOOK

THE LITTLE PINK BOOK

Quotations on Women

Compiled, Annotated
& Introduced by

OLINE LUINENBURG
& STEPHEN OSBORNE

A LITTLE RED BOOK
ARSENAL PULP PRESS

A LITTLE RED BOOK

THE LITTLE PINK BOOK:
QUOTATIONS ON WOMEN
Copyright ©1990
by Arsenal Pulp Press Ltd.
All Rights Reserved
ISBN 0-88978-226-1
Third printing: 1992

CIP Data: See page 6

LITTLE RED BOOKS ARE
PUBLISHED BY
ARSENAL PULP PRESS
1062 Homer Street #100
Vancouver BC V6B 2W9

Cover: Kelly Brooks
Illustration: Eve Corbel
Typesetting: Vancouver Desktop
Publishing Centre
Printing: Webcom
Printed and bound in Canada

TABLE OF CONTENTS

CANADIAN CATALOGUING IN
PUBLICATION DATA

Main entry under title:
Little pink book
  ISBN 0-88978-226-1
   1. Women—Quotations. 2. Women—
Humor. 3. Quotations, English.
I. Luinenberg, Oline, 1962- II. Osborne,
J. S. (James Stephen), 1947-
PN6084.W6L5 1990   305.4'0207
C90-091704-0

INTRODUCTION

From Cleopatra to Margaret Thatcher, the illustrious and the not-so-illustrious have been led freely—at times, perhaps, wantonly—to speculate on the inner nature and the outward role of women in the various societies of the western world. In the last two thousand-odd years much has been said about the larger half of humankind, and much of that has been written down—so much that we are led to wonder whether there has been anyone anywhere who did not offer an opinion on this subject, however ill-considered or well-articulated.

With this present volume—a distillation of twenty-four centuries of rumination, rumour, fulmination and remark—we hope to offer our readers an historical perspective that might assist them in fashioning fresh utterances on this perennially interesting subject, or at least to avoid unnecessarily repeating what has already been said—and perhaps thereby to avoid repeating history itself.

Where possible, we have supplied with each quotation a date or approximation thereof; where no date could be found, we have elected nevertheless to include material deemed especially relevant when it is corroborated by the sources.

ON UNLEASHING THE
STRENGTH OF WOMEN

A woman is like a teabag—only in hot water do you realize how strong she is.

—Nancy Reagan

ON THE ADVANTAGES
OF BEING A WOMAN

I'd much rather be a woman than a man. Women can cry, they can wear cute clothes, and they're the first to be rescued off sinking ships.

—Gilda Radner, 1979

STRONG ADVICE WITH CAVEAT

Don't accept rides from strange men, and remember that all men are strange as hell.

—Robin Morgan

A CERTAIN VISION OF PERFECTION

The perfect woman has a brilliant brain, wants to make love until four in the morning—and then turns into a pizza.

—*David Lee Roth,
rock singer, 1988*

NOW LET ME MAKE MYSELF
PERFECTLY CLEAR

I want to make a policy statement. I am unabashedly in favor of women.

—*Herbert Hoover,
U.S. President, 1929*

ON WHAT MEN ARE INEXPLICABLY
PROUD OF

It is funny the two things most men are proudest of is the thing that any man can do and does in the same way, that is being drunk and being the father of their son.

—*Gertrude Stein*

ON THE WRONG AND THE RIGHT OF IT, IN THAT ORDER

When women go wrong, men go right after them.

—*Mae West*

ON THE ADMONISHMENT OF WIVES AND THE QUESTION OF WHATEVER SHE IS SUPPOSED TO DO

How is a person to admonish his wife if she goes out on the town with other people, to wit, guys, drinking, and comes home late when she should have been looking

after the children or cooking, or whatever she is supposed to do?
—*Manitoba judge, 1989*

ON THERE BEING NOT MUCH LEFT TO FIGHT FOR

The battle for women's rights has been largely won.
—*Margaret Thatcher, 1982*

BUT LET ME MAKE ONE THING PERFECTLY CLEAR

I owe nothing to Women's Lib.
—*Margaret Thatcher, 1982*

ON BEING DAMN PROUD OF IT

I am not in any way, shape, or form a feminist. My first job was in a battery factory where I was paid less than the man next to me, operating the same machine. I quit—but it didn't sour me or turn me into a radical feminist. I simply learned that God helps those who help themselves.

—*Dorothy Dobbie, ex-pres.*
Winnipeg Chamber of
Commerce, 1989

ON THE QUALIFICATIONS, NOT TO
MENTION THE GENDER, OF THE
SUPREME BEING

The Yale president must be a Yale man. Not too far to the right, too far to the left or a middle-of-the-roader. You may have guessed who the leading candidate is, but there is a question about him: Is God a Yale man?

—*Wilmorth S. Lewis, Yale*

ON THE EDUCATION OF
WOMEN IN POLITICS

Give them a few months on the Hill. It's amazing how immersion in that male world educates women who start off wincing at the feminist label.

—*Jocelyne Cote-O'Hara,*
policy adviser to Brian Mulroney,
1983-86, 1989

ON THE POSSIBILITY OF ACHIEVING
ANOTHER STATE

A man wants his virility regarded, a woman wants her femininity appreciated, however indirect and subtle the indications of regard and appreciation. On [the planet] Winter they will not exist. One is respected and judged as a human

being. It is an appalling experience.
—*From* The Left Hand of
Darkness, *by Ursula LeGuin*

ON GRAVITY AS AN ALTERNATIVE
TO THE OBSTETRICIAN

There are women who like to be
allowed to be women, who like to
have their babies *with* gravity in-
stead of against it to please some
obstetrician.
—*Margaret Mead, 1978*

ON THE INEVITABILITY OF
UNDESIRABLE ENDINGS

"I hate discussions of feminism
that end up with who does the
dishes," she said. So do I. But at the
end, there are always the dammed
dishes.

ON FINDING A NEW SOLUTION TO SQUARE PEGS AND ROUND HOLES

Freud's basic view was that every woman was a square peg trying to fit into a round hole. It did not occur to him that it might be less destructive to change the shape of the holes rather than to knock all the corners off.

—*Eva Figes, 1970*

DIALECTICAL UNDERCURRENTS

Some of us are becoming the men we wanted to marry.

—*Gloria Steinem, 1981*

ON SETTING PRIORITIES
IN THE MEDICAL PROFESSION

If you have a psychotic fixation and you go to the doctor and you want those two fingers amputated, he will not cut them off. But he will remove your genitals. I have more trouble getting a prescription for Valium than I do having my uterus lowered and made into a penis.

—*Lily Tomlin, 1974*

NOT TO PUT TOO FINE
A POINT ON IT

The definition of woman's work is shitwork.

—*Gloria Steinem, 1974*

YES, BUT HOW MANY FIT
IN A VOLKSWAGEN?

Women are like elephants to me, they're nice to look at but I wouldn't want to own one.
— *W.C. Fields*

ON STARTING WITH THE BASIC
QUALITIES OF THE MALE EGO

The male ego with few exceptions is elephantine to start with.
— *Bette Davis, 1962*

ON THE ENLARGING ASPECT
OF WOMEN

Women have served all these centuries as looking glasses possessing the magic and delicious power of

reflecting the figure of man at twice
its natural size.
—*Virginia Woolf, 1933*

ON WOMEN AS LOWEST COMMON DENOMINATOR

I used to tell my husband that, if he
could make *me* understand some-
thing, it would be clear to all the
other people in the country.
—*Eleanor Roosevelt, 1947*

ON THE IRREVERSIBLE ASPECTS OF DISCRIMINATION AGAINST MEN

Women's liberation is just a lot of
foolishness. It's the men who are
discriminated against. They can't
bear children. And no one's likely
to do anything about that.
—*Golda Meir, 1972*

YOUNG WOMAN'S BLUES

No time to marry, no time to settle down; I'm a young woman, and I ain't done runnin aroun'.

—*Bessie Smith, 1927*

ON ELIMINATING THE DOUBLE STANDARD

I believe in the single standard for men and women.

—*Mae West*

MOTHERHOOD OVER CITIZENHOOD

The insistence that the woman as a mother prevails over the woman as citizen at least puts a slight drag upon agitation for war.

—*Margaret Mead, 1935*

ON THE SUITABILITY OF
BRAINS FOR WOMEN

I had no reason to doubt that brains were suitable for a woman. And as I had my father's kind of mind—which was also his mother's—I learned that the mind is not sex-typed.

—*Margaret Mead, 1972*

ON THE GETTING OF BRAINS

You know women don't get much brains before they're 30 anyway, but at the age of 18 or so they make some stupid mistakes, mostly because we males, who know better, lead them to it.

—*Les Bewley, B.C. judge, 1988*

ON THE SPECIAL QUALITIES
OF WOMEN

I appreciate the intuitive talents that women can bring to the decision-making process.
—*Bill Vander Zalm, B.C. Premier*

ON DAUGHTERS AND
THEIR FATHERS

My father [Pandit Jawaharlal Nehru] was a statesman, I'm a political woman. My father was a saint. I'm not.
—*Indira Gandhi, 1975*

ON THE NATURE OF HUSBANDS

Husbands are like fires. They go out when unattended.
—*Zsa Zsa Gabor, 1960*

ON THE SALUBRIOUS EFFECT OF
BEING SPOKEN ILL OF

Do you know, it is not praise that does me good, but when men speak ill of me, then, with a noble assurance I say to myself, as I smile at them, "let us be revenged by proving them to be liars."

> —*Catherine II, Empress of Russia, late 18th century*

ON THE SIGNIFICANCE OF
LONGEVITY, OR ITS LACK

Man is more robust than woman, but he is not longer lived; which exactly explains my view of their attachments.

> —*Jane Austen, circa 1800*

ON THE RELATIVE LONGEVITY OF MALE AND FEMALE TV NEWS ANNOUNCERS

I think our shelf-life is a little shorter. I use the term "best before date."

—*Pamela Wallin, CTV News*

ON WHAT A LADY ALWAYS DOES

What did she say? Just what she ought, of course. A lady always does.

—*Jane Austen, circa 1800*

ON WHAT A WOMAN CANNOT BE MORE THAN

You may be a princess or the richest woman in the world, but you cannot be more than a lady.

—*Jennie Churchill, 1908*

ON DRAWING THE LINE

I will *not* be exhibited in his Triumph!

—*Cleopatra, 30 BC*

ON THE EQUALITY
OF UNHAPPINESS

Nuns and married women are equally unhappy, if in different ways.

—*Queen Christina of Sweden,*
mid 17th century

ON BEING OVER THIRTY YEARS
OF AGE AND FINDING IT
MUCH LESS DIFFICULT

As you know, no one over thirty years of age is afraid of tittle-tattle.

I myself find it much less difficult to strangle a man than to fear him.
—*Queen Christina of Sweden, mid 17th century*

ON THE WHERE AND WHAT OF A WOMAN'S PLACE

A woman's place is in the home looking after the family, not out working.
—*Pope John Paul II, 1981*

ON THE RIGHT OF WOMEN TO WORK

They have a right to work wherever they want to—as long as they have dinner ready when you get home.
—*John Wayne*

ON UNDERSTANDING THE
IMPLICATIONS OF THE RIGHT OF
WOMEN TO WORK

Strange to say, even when men are willing for their wives to take on public work, they never seem to understand that this cannot always be done between mealtimes.
—*Hannah Mitchell, 1968*

ON WHO WEARS THE PANTS
IN MRS. THATCHER'S HOUSE

I do, and I also wash and iron them.
—*Denis Thatcher, 1981*

ON THERE BEING
SOMETHING AT LEAST
OR SOME TO BE
THANKFUL FOR

I thank God I am not a woman, to be

touched with so many giddy offenses as he hath generally taxed their whole sex withal.

—*From* As You Like It,
by William Shakespeare

ON IMPERFECTION,
MISPERFECTION
AND THE HUMID WIND
FROM THE SOUTH

In her particular nature, woman is defective and misbegotten, for the active force in the male seed tends to the production of a perfect likeness in the masculine sex; while the production of woman is due to a weakness in the generative force or imperfection in the pre-existing matter or even from some external

influences, for example, the humid
winds from the south.
> —*St. Thomas Aquinas,
> mid 13th century*

ON RECOMMENDED CAUTIONS

As a recommended caution, a
woman must stand behind a man
and the place of her prostration be
located a little behind that of the
man.
> —*Ayatollah Khomeini, 1980*

ON THE GENDER-SPECIFIC
QUALITIES OF DEEDS
AND WORDS

Words are women, deeds are men.
> —*George Herbert,
> early 17th century*

THE TRUTH ABOUT GETTING
THINGS DONE

In politics if you want anything said, ask a man. If you want anything done, ask a woman.

—*Margaret Thatcher*

ON EXPECTED
SIDE-EFFECTS OF THE
SUFFRAGIST MOVEMENT

Give women the vote, and in five years there will be a crushing tax on bachelors.

—*George Bernard Shaw,
circa 1914*

INTIMATIONS OF DIRE
CONSEQUENCE FROM MR. ASQUITH

The grant of the Parliamentary franchise to women in this country would be a political mistake of a very disastrous kind.

—H.S. Asquith,
British Prime Minister

ON THE BRITISH PRIME MINISTER, MR. ASQUITH

Undistinguished in his crimes, expedited by his clumsy thwackings of women from behind the bars of authority.

—Rebecca West

ON INNOVATION, AND BEING PREPARED FOR ONE

The appointment of a woman to office is an innovation for which the public is not prepared. Nor am I.

—Thomas Jefferson,
late 18th century

TACTICAL CONSIDERATIONS OF A WOMAN RUNNING FOR PARTY LEADERSHIP

Well, I thought about running as a man, but I decided against it.
—*Audrey McLaughlin,*
NDP Leader, 1989

A LITTLE KNOWN ASPECT OF THE WOMEN'S MOVEMENT

The history of men's opposition to women's emancipation is more interesting perhaps than the story of that emancipation itself.
—*Virginia Woolf, 1933*

ON MAD WICKED FOLLY AND HORRORS, HEARTLESSNESS, FEELING AND PROPRIETY

The Queen is most anxious to enlist everyone who can speak or write to join in checking this mad, wicked folly of "Women's Rights," with all its attendant horrors on which her poor feeble sex is bent, forgetting every sense of womanly feeling and propriety. Woman would become the most hateful, heartless and disgusting of human beings were she allowed to unsex herself; and where would be the protection which man was intended to give the weaker sex?

—*Queen Victoria,*
late 19th century

ON JUST WHAT CONSTITUTES A YOUNG PLAYER, THESE DAYS

There's nothing wrong with the ladies, God bless them; let them play. But what they're doing is eliminating much of the available time when young players can get on the course.

—*Jack Nicklaus, golfer, 1978*

ON THE DISTINCTION BETWEEN REASON AND EMOTION, WITH A BOW TO IMMEASURABLE NEW REALMS AND STABLE ELEMENTS

Woman and man represent two quite different types of being. Reason is dominant in man. He searches, analyses and often opens new immeasurable realms. But all these things that he approaches merely by reason are subject to change. Feeling in contrast is much more stable than reason and woman is the feeling and therefore the stable element.

—*Adolf Hitler, 1936*

ON THE JUSTICE OF SENTENCING A CRIMINAL TO 120 DAYS IN LOCAL JAIL FOR RAPING AND BEATING A WOMAN

He would stand the chance of violent sexual abuse and becoming a homosexual if sent to a state prison.

—*Robert C. Abel,*
U.S. judge, 1982

ON TAKING BACK THE NIGHT

Once in cabinet we had to deal with the fact that there had been an outbreak of assaults on women at night. One minister suggested a curfew: women should stay home after dark. I said, "But it's the men who are attacking the women. If there's to be a curfew, let the men stay home, not the women."

—*Golda Meir, 1974*

FOR BETTER OR WORSE: ON THE
INEXORABLE COURSE OF THINGS

Woman is more impressionable than man. Therefore in the Golden Age they were better than men; now they are worse.

—*Count Leo Tolstoy,
late 19th century*

ON THE SOUL OF MAN, AND WHAT'S GOOD FOR IT

A little bit of rape is good for man's soul.

—*Norman Mailer, 1972*

ON DEFORMITIES AS THEY OCCUR IN THE ORDINARY STATE OF NATURE

We should look upon the female state as it were a deformity, though one that occurs in the ordinary course of nature.

—*Aristotle, 4th century BC*

ON WHAT MOST WOMEN ARE—AN ARISTOCRATIC VIEW

Most women are bird-brained. It's rare to find a woman with very good mental agility.

—*Earl Spencer, father of the
Princess of Wales, 1987*

ON THE ELIMINATION OF
UNEMPLOYMENT, DIVORCE,
DELINQUENCY AND OTHER EVILS

If we had more feminine women
there would be less unemploy-
ment, divorce, delinquency and
other evils.

—*Isabelle Stayt, Campaign for
the Feminine Woman, 1983*

ON WHAT RICH WIDOWS ARE—
A MERCANTILE VIEW

Rich widows are only second-hand
goods that sell at first class prices.

—*Benjamin Franklin,
late 18th century*

ON THE IMMENSE WORK
STILL AWAITING MAN

Three things have been difficult to tame: the oceans, fools and women. We may soon be able to tame the ocean; fools and women will take a little longer.

—*Spiro Agnew, 1970*

ON WHAT WOMEN MIGHT OR
MIGHT NOT BE EXPECTED TO DO

Women should not be expected to write, or fight, or build, or compose scores; she does all by inspiring men to do all.

—*Ralph Waldo Emerson,
mid 19th century*

ON WHAT WOMEN CANNOT DO

No woman can paint.
  —*John Ruskin, late 19th century*

ON WHAT WOMEN CAN DO

There's only one woman I know who could never be a symphony conductor, and that's the Venus de Milo.

  —*Margaret Hillis, Director,*
  Chicago Symphony Orchestra

ON MAKING CHOICES

Did anyone tell Toscanini, or Bach, that he had to choose between music and family, between art and a normal life?
  —*Elisabeth Mann Borgese, 1963*

ON WHEN
THE HONEYMOON BEGINS

I have a very clear, keen memory of myself the day after I was married. I was sweeping a floor.
> —*Adrienne Rich, 1976*

ON DRAWING INFERENCES FROM
THE BOOK OF GENESIS

"Adam was first formed, then Eve." What does that prove? Either nothing, or that man is inferior to the fishes.
> —*Lillie Devereux Blake, 1883*

ON BEAUTY, WONDER,
ADMIRABLENESS
AND DIVINITY ITSELF

Nothing can compare in beauty and wonder and admirableness and divinity itself, to the silent work in obscure dwellings of faithful women bringing their children to honour and virtue and piety.

—Henry Ward Beecher,
mid 19th century

ON THE UTILITY OF ADVERTISING SLOGANS IN UNDERSTANDING WOMEN

That the child is the supreme aim of woman is a statement having precisely the value of an advertising slogan.

—Simone de Beauvoir, 1952

SAD BUT TRUE

There is no bar mitzvah for menopause.

—Pauline Bart, 1971

ON HAVING A GOOD LAUGH

If ever you want a really good laugh, read up some of the incredibly involved and convoluted arguments of a male evolutionist trying to explain why women, alone of all primates, equipped herself with a hymen, which appears on the face of it to have no other purpose than to keep him out.

—*Elaine Morgan, 1972*

ON EXCEPTIONS
THAT PROVE THE RULE

Love is the only circumstance in which the female is pardoned for sexual activity.

—*Kate Millett, 1970*

ON THE ETERNAL QUESTION

"Love" is the woman's pitiful deluded attempt to attain the human.
—*Ti-Grace Atkinson, 1969*

WELL, IF YOU'RE GOING TO GO AHEAD ANYWAY

Go ahead and *love!* we say to women. But don't get so excited about it.
—*Ruth Herschberger, 1948*

ON THE FIRST WOMAN GOD EVER MADE

If de fust woman God ever made was strong enough to turn de world upside down all 'lone, dese togedder ought to be able to turn it back

again, and now dey asking to do it,
de men better let 'em.
—*Sojourner Truth,
anti-slavery activist, 1851*

ON THE NEED FOR
DIRECT ACTION

Ef women want any rights more'n
dey's got, why don't dey jes' take
'em, and not be talkin' about it.
—*Sojourner Truth, 1863*

PROUD TO BE PART
OF THE PROBLEM

I proudly love being a Negro
woman. It's so involved and interesting. We are the problem—the
great national game of taboo.

—*Anne Spencer,
poet, activist, 1927*

ON MEN WITHOUT WOMEN

A man without a woman is like a vase without flowers.

> —*proverb, Cape Verde Island*

ON THE OTHER HAND

A woman without a man is like a fish without a bicycle.

> —*Gloria Steinem*

HOW MEN COOPERATE
WITH WOMEN

Women want mediocre men, and men are working to be as mediocre as possible.

> —*Margaret Mead*

ON MEN IN LOVE

A man in love is incomplete until he is married. Then he's finished.
　　　　　　　—*Zsa Zsa Gabor, 1960*

ON THE RAISING OF
THE MINDS OF MEN

Man's minds are raised to the level of the women with whom they associate.

　　　　　　　—*Alexander Dumas,*
　　　　　　　French novelist, 1830

ON WHO GETS THE BLAME

All that I am my mother made me.
　　　　　　　—*John Quincy Adams,*
　　　　　　　early 19th century

ON SOME SMALL SATISFACTION

So mothers have God's license to be

missed.
> —*Elizabeth Barrett Browning,*
> *mid 19th century*

ON BEARING BOYS INTO
THE BEST FORTUNE

Give me the life of the boy whose mother is nurse, seamstress, washerwoman, cook, teacher, angel and saint, all in one, and whose father is guide, exemplar, and friend. No servants to come between. These are the boys who are born to the best fortune.

> —*Andrew Carnegie*

ON THE VISITING OF
VIRTUE AND SIN

I think it must be somewhere written, that the virtues of mothers shall be visited on their children, as well as the sins of the fathers.

—*Charles Dickens*

ON THE PRESENCE OF THE CHERISHED CHILD

The mother's yearning, that completed type of love within another life which is the essence of human love, feels the presence of the cherished child, even in the base degraded man.

—*George Eliot*

ON LAST DITCH EXPEDIENTS

God could not be everywhere, and therefore He made mothers.

—*Jewish homily*

ON THE SOURCE OF
REAL WEALTH

No man is poor who has had a godly mother.

—*Abraham Lincoln*

CREDIT WHERE CREDIT IS DUE

All that I am or hope to be I owe to my mother.

—*Abraham Lincoln*

ON THE FUTURE GLORY
OF FRANCE

France needs nothing so much to promote her regeneration as good mothers.

—*Napoleon Bonaparte*

ON JUST WHO IS RESPONSIBLE FOR FUTURE GENERATIONS

Into the woman's keeping is committed the destiny of the generations to come after us.

— *Theodore Roosevelt*

A DEBT SO RARELY PAID

My mother was the most beautiful woman I ever saw. All I am I owe to my mother.

— *George Washington*

ON TRAGEDY IN A GENDER-SPECIFIC WORLD

All women become like their mothers. That is their tragedy. No man does. That is his.

— *Oscar Wilde*

ON THE ROAD NOT
TRAVELLED BY

Sometimes when I look at all my children, I say to myself, "Lillian, you should have stayed a virgin."
—*Lillian Carter, mother of U.S. president Jimmy Carter*

ON THE PROPER FUNCTION
OF WOMEN

I should like to know what is the proper function of women, if it is not to make reasons for husbands to stay at home, and still stronger reasons for bachelors to go out.
—*From* The Mill on the Floss, *by George Eliot*

ON NURSES, PORTERS, HORSES AND POLICEMEN

No *man*, not even a doctor, ever gives any other definition of what a nurse should be than this—"devoted and obedient." This definition would do just as well for a porter. It might even do for a horse. It would not do for a policeman.

—*Florence Nightingale, 1859*

ON ELOPEMENT, DIVORCE AND KINDNESS

We don't elope nowadays, and we don't divorce, except out of kindness.

—*Jennie Churchill, 1913*

ON PASSING THROUGH CRISIS

When a woman ceases to alter the

fashion of her hair, you guess that she has passed the crisis of her experience.

—*Mary Hunter Austin,*
suffragist, 1903

ON SUFFRAGISTS AND HAIRSTYLES

I am opposed by all short-haired women and long-haired men in the province.

—*R.P. Roblin,*
Manitoba premier, 1912

ON HAIR COLOUR
AND EXCITEMENT

An exciting party should have both blondes and brunettes.

—*Pierre Elliott Trudeau, 1968*

ON THE IMPORTANCE OF
PARTICULAR CASES

What is sauce for the goose may be sauce for the gander, but it is not necessarily sauce for the chicken, the duck, the turkey, or the guinea hen.

—*Alice B. Toklas, 1954*

ON THE IMPORTANCE OF NEVER
TURNING YOUR BACK

In passing, also, I would like to say that the first time Adam had a chance he laid the blame on woman.

—*Nancy Astor, first woman to sit in British House of Commons, 1923*

ON FIGHTING THE SYSTEM, 1955

My vigor, vitality and cheek repel
me. I am the kind of woman I would
run from.

> —*Nancy Astor, 1955*

ON FIGHTING THE SYSTEM, 1790

It is very hard that a pretty woman
is never to be told she is so by any of
her own sex without that person's
being suspected to be either her de-
termined Enemy, or her professed
Toadeater.

> —*Jane Austen, 1790*

ON SETTLING FOR THE LESSER EVIL

Without thinking highly either of
men or of matrimony, marriage had
always been her object; it was the
only honourable provision for well-

educated young women of small fortune, and however uncertain of giving happiness, must be their pleasantest preservative from want.
—*from* Pride and Prejudice,
by Jane Austen

ON EQUAL OPPORTUNITY
IN THE 17TH CENTURY

How comes it to passe, that when a Father hath a numerous issue of Sonnes and Daughters, the sonnes forsooth are trained up in the Liberall Arts and Sciences, and there (if they prove not Block-heads) they may in time be book-learned while we are set onely to the Needle, to prick our fingers: or else to the Wheele to spinne a faire thread for our owne undoings.

—Mary Tattlewell, (pseudonym). From Epistle to the Reader: Long Megge of Westminster, hearing the abuse, offeres to women to riseth out of her grave and thus speaketh in The Women's Sharpe Revenge: or an Answer to Sir Seldome Sober that writ those railing Pamphelets called The Juniper and The Crab-Tree Lectures, etc. Being a sound Reply and a full Confutation of those Bookes: in this case for the Defense of us Women, with Joane Hit-him-Home, *1640*

WHAT MEN HAVE FORGOTTEN

What men have forgotten and what they don't want to know is that we are *animals*.

—Dora Russell

AND CONTINUE TO FORGET

Human beings are not animals, and

I do not want to see sex and sexual differences treated as casually and amorally as dogs and other beasts treat them. I believe this could happen under the ERA.

—*Ronald Reagan*

WELL, MAYBE, BUT THERE'S STILL A CATCH

A woman is but an animal, and an animal not of the highest order.

—*Edmund Burke, 18th century*

OR AT ANY OTHER MOMENT, WE SUPPOSE

Louise Brough cannot serve at this moment because she has not got any balls.

—*Rex Alston,*
tennis commentator, 1988

INSIDE THE WORLD OF SPORT, IN A GRAMSCIAN SENSE

Sport is an armoured apparatus for coercion, an instrument of bourgeois hegemony in a Gramscian sense, dominated by a phallocratic and fascistoid idea of virility.

—*Jean-Marie Brohm,
French coach, 1988*

INVESTIGATION INTO CONDITIONS FAVOURABLE FOR BICYCLE RIDING

There is no reason to think a healthy woman can be injured while riding a bicycle, provided she does not over-exert herself by riding too long a time, or too fast, or up too steep hills, and provided she does not ride when common sense and

physiology alike forbid any need-
less exertion.

—Dr. J. West Roosevelt,
from "A Doctor's View
of Bicycling," Scribner's, 1895

INVESTIGATION INTO PERCEPTIONS
FAVOURABLE FOR BICYCLE RIDING

What was once frowned down upon
as unladylike, trivial and shocking,
is now done openly and with the
approval of the beholders. Perhaps
nothing illustrates this so much as
the riding of the bicycle.

—Dr. Gracie Ritchie, National
Council of Women of Canada
Yearbook, 1895

ON GETTING SERIOUS,
FOR GODSSAKE

Would men have us run races with a powder puff in one hand and a mirror in the other?

> —*Roxy Atkins, U.S. champion hurdler, late 1930s*

THE PRO-CHOICE MOVEMENT AND THE TEARING DOWN OF METAPHORICAL WALLS

The senseless termination of human life at the slightest whim or notion of women is simply removing yet another stone from the wall of an already crumbling society.

> —*Bill Vander Zalm, B.C. Premier, 1988*

ON WHAT WOMEN'S CENTRES
REALLY ARE

By and large nothing more than drop-in centres disseminating a lot of anti-government, feminist literature.

—*Peggy Steacy,*
REAL Women, 1990

ON FACING IT
IN REAL LIFE

It was lovely to see so many Real members at the Pro-Life dinner dance, always one of the happiest events of the year—it is so relaxing to be with like-minded people— let's face it, pro-lifers are nicer people!

—*Peggy Steacy,*
REAL Women, 1990

THRILL-SEEKING
ALTERNATIVES REMAIN

Life in this society being, at best, an utter bore and no aspect of society being at all relevant to women, there remains to civic-minded, responsible, thrill-seeking females only to overthrow the government, eliminate the money system, institute complete automation and destroy the male sex.

—*Valerie Solanis, the woman who shot Andy Warhol*

ON WHAT MIGHT BE PREFERABLE TO SENDING A WOMAN TV CORRESPONDENT ON FOREIGN ASSIGNMENT WITH A MAN

Changing the cameraman was bet-

ter than having some broad along.
—*Anne Medina, CBC announcer*
and foreign correspondent

ON THE SIMILARITY BETWEEN WOMEN AND RULES

Rules are like women, they're made to be violated.

—*Denys Dionne,*
Quebec judge, 1990

ON WHAT MEN HAVE TO PROTECT THEMSELVES AGAINST

. . . it appears that this three-year-old girl was sexually aggressive.
—*Judge Vander Hoop, 1989*

ON THE IMPLICATIONS OF SEX EDUCATION IN THE SCHOOLS

I'm not so sure if I want some

woman in a low slung blouse standing in front of a bunch of grade 12 students giving long dissertations on rape . . . maybe I'm just a dirty old man.

—*Mel Couvelier,*
Mayor, Saanich, B.C., 1979

ON THE DEEPER IMPLICATIONS OF SEX EDUCATION IN THE SCHOOLS

Yes, Mayor Couvelier, you are a dirty old man.

—*S.L. Murphy,*
Victoria Rape Relief, 1979

ON FREE-STANDING SUPPORT FOR SINGLE MOTHERS

Well, certainly, if one of those single mothers on welfare finds herself pregnant with an unwanted child, I think that she should find relief by going to any of our free-standing churches and ridding herself of her unchristian feelings of depression.

—*Bill Vander Zalm,*
B.C. Premier, 1988

THE SURPRISING THING ABOUT PREGNANCY

I've gone through it four times and it's been a very enjoyable experience.

—*Peter Dueck,*
B.C. Health Minister, 1988

ON ABORTION AND ANYTHING YOU WANT

It is immoral, unchristian, anti-social, inhuman and against anything you want. All Liberal

members are in favour of that.
—*Henri Latulippe, Quebec MP*
(Creditiste), 1988

ON NATURAL BELIEFS

Woman must understand that maternity is a natural creed and that all in all, it is a good thing for her.
—*André Fortin, Quebec MP*

WELL, IF IT'S OBVIOUS TO THE PRESIDENT ...

I've noticed that everybody that is for abortion has already been born.
—*Ronald Reagan*

ON WHY PREGNANT WOMEN CANNOT DECIDE FOR THEMSELVES

We have only to remember the peculiar behaviour of a pregnant woman. She is somewhat disturbed and her reasoning and judgement are not as logical as in other circumstances.

—*Rene Matte, Quebec MP*

ON JUST WHAT THE TAXPAYER IS NOT RESPONSIBLE FOR

Not many people will argue with your statement about a woman's right to choose abortion. However, most people . . . would not agree that it is the responsibility of the taxpayers of America to fund a woman's choice, which may have been brought about by her excesses, indiscretions, carelessness, fornication, adultery, etc.

—*Samuel L. Devine, U.S Congress*

ON MALE POLITICIANS WHO CHARGE THEMSELVES WITH THE SETTLEMENT OF WOMEN'S ISSUES

Such flunky minds, affected at birth with an incremental lack of dignity, must invariably be attracted by the elaborate, insincere ceremony of party politics.

—*Rebecca West*

ON DEPICTING GRISLY MURDERS OF WOMEN IN THE MOVIES

Its a sad state of affairs when you can't make a murder mystery and kill anybody because you're going to offend a small group.

—*Brian de Palma, 1990*

ON THE ROOT CAUSE OF THE
MONTREAL MASSACRE

Anti-male hatred creates this kind of rage.

—*Ross Virgin,
Toronto men's group, 1990*

ON JUST WHAT MIGHT HAVE
TRIGGERED THE TERRIBLE RESPONSE
OF MASS MURDERER MARC LEPINE

He just might have been a man whose child had been aborted by a feminist, and that might have been enough to trigger the terrible response.

—*Peggy Steacy, REAL Women,
Newsletter (postage paid by B.C.
government)*

ON ASSAULTING WOMEN, AND THE INFLUENCE OF FEMINISTS AND STALINISTS

Assaulted women like being beaten . . . and I tell the guy to hit harder. If they go to court, these men have no chance. There is no justice. Feminists and Stalinists have influence on the judges.

—*Police officer quoted by N.B. Council on the Status of Women*

ON WHERE TO TURN AFTER EVENTS LIKE THE MONTREAL MASSACRE

During such intense moments, it is important, more than ever, to turn to the word of God.

—*Paul Cardinal Gregoire, archbishop of Montreal, 1989*

ON WHAT TO EXPECT HAVING
TURNED TO THE WORD OF GOD

My own Catholic church is one of the last bastions of sexism.

> —*Jean Ann Ledwell,*
> *Montreal nun, 1989*

SOME THOUGHTS ON SUFFERING

Certainly those that suffer, say from the pressure of unwanted pregnancy, will find it much, much easier to cope with the situation if they have a faith in Jesus Christ.

> —*Bill Vander Zalm,*
> *B.C. Premier, 1988*

ON THE LIFE OF RILEY

The mature bohemian is one whose woman works full time.

> —*North Beach homily*

THOUGHTS ON AUTO-SEMINATION

If I had a cock for a day I would get myself pregnant.

—*Germaine Greer*

ON THE DIVINE INTENTION

If God had wanted us to think with our wombs, why would He give us a brain?

—*Claire Booth Luce*

ON WHAT WOMEN OUGHT NOT TO HAVE, AND WHY

Women have, or ought to have, but little liberty; they are apt to indulge themselves excessively in what is allowed them.

—*Jean Jacques Rousseau, 18th century*

"A FIRST BLAST OF THE TRUMPET AGAINST THE MONSTROUS REGIMENT OF WOMEN"

To promote a Woman to bear rule, superiority, dominion, or empire, above any Realm, Nation or City, is repugnant to Nature; contrary to God, a thing most contrarious to his revealed will and approved ordinance; and finally it is the subversion of good order, of all equity and justice.

—*John Knox, founder, Presbyterian Church, 1558*

ON WHAT BRITAIN NEEDS

What Britain needs is an iron lady.
—*Margaret Thatcher*

ON HAVING SECOND THOUGHTS
ABOUT WOMEN PRIESTS

I used to be in favour of women priests but two years in Margaret Thatcher's Cabinet cured me of it.
—*Norman St.John-Stevas, 1981*

ON WHAT TO EXPECT AT THE END
OF THE RAINBOW

I have sacrificed everything in my life that I consider precious in order to advance the political career of my husband.

—*Pat Nixon*

ON HAVING EQUAL RIGHTS
WITH MERE MEN

Well, it's hard for a mere man to

believe that woman doesn't already have equal rights.

—*Dwight D. Eisenhower*

ON WOMEN IN THE PROFESSIONS

I consider that women who are authors, lawyers and politicians are monsters.

—*Pierre Auguste Renoir*

ON BECOMING A FEMINIST

I became a feminist as an alternative to becoming a masochist.

—*Sally Kempton*

INSTEAD OF A DOORMAT

People call me a feminist whenever I express sentiments that differentiate me from a doormat.

—*Rebecca West*

SOME MIGHT SAY OVER-EXPLOITED

Women—the greatest undeveloped natural resource in the world today.
—*Edward Steichen*

ON THE NECESSITY OF
DOING TWICE AS WELL

Whatever women do, they must do twice as well as men to be thought half as good. Luckily, this is not difficult.

—*Charlotte Whitton,
mayor of Ottawa*

ON IMAGINATION

Women have more imagination than men. They need it to tell us how wonderful we are.
—*Arnold Glasgow*

ON THE DESIRE TO MAKE ALL
WOMEN BEAUTIFUL

My dream is to save them from nature.

—*Christian Dior*

ON WHAT MIGHT KEEP ONE AWAKE
ALL THESE YEARS

The great question that has never been answered and which I have not yet been able to answer despite my thirty years of research into the feminine soul is: What does a woman want?

—*Sigmund Freud*

Why are women so much more interesting to men than men are to women?

—*Virginia Woolf, 1933*

Index

81

OLINE LUINENBURG is an editor and a graduate student in Communications at Simon Fraser University, Vancuver.

STEPHEN OSBORNE is co-editor of *Quotations of Chairman Zalm* and publisher of *Geist* Magazine.